How to Handle Rejection

*The Ultimate Guide
to Dealing with Rejection
and Conquering
the Fear of Rejection
for Good*

by Patrick McIntyre

Table of Contents

Introduction

There are many ways to be rejected, unfortunately, and none of them feel good. Some even impact our pockets, especially when we fail to get that job, promotion, sale, or much-needed loan. Still others have a negative impact on our lifestyles, such as being denied housing.

While those are bad enough, there's also the agony of being rejected by someone we feel we just can't live without. There's a reason so many books, movies, and songs are about unrequited love — almost all of us can relate to them. For as long as people have been telling stories and writing them down, being rejected by someone who makes our hearts go on overdrive is a terrible pain that has happened in every era and in all cultures.

Even more unfortunate, rejection is an inherent part of life. While most people are able to pick themselves up eventually, others develop such an overriding fear of rejection that they stop trying to reach out for more.

As a result, they settle down in their dead-end jobs, afraid to ask for a raise or promotion, or are even afraid to quit and try out with another company. They settle down with their passionless, dead-end relationship; or equally worse, become recluses, afraid to reach out for fear of being rejected again.

While not denying that there are benefits to a stable job, one can also argue that sticking to one because of fear is not healthy, either. The same goes for staying in a joyless relationship, or equally worse, avoiding all relationships outright.

Living in fear is not healthy, but some fears have a use. Certain fears can actually protect us from shady characters, places, and situations, so long as it does not become our overriding emotion. Living in fear of rejection, however, has no survival value whatsoever. Living this way is a form of self-sabotage, a kind of slow suicide, if you will.

In this book we'll explore why people are so afraid of rejection, and the latest studies on the matter, which suggest there could actually be biological reasons for it. Then we'll explain how to deal with rejection in a relationship, as well as in a career in sales.

Considering our topic, we'll also look into the mechanics behind our aversion to failure and rejection, and equally important, how to manage fear so you can move past it. Finally, we'll explain how to overcome the fear of rejection for good.

What are we waiting for? Let's get started!

Chapter 1: Why Are People Afraid of Rejection?

Besides the fact that it hurts, you mean? Well, it's also humiliating, you must admit. Those factors aside, there's a growing body of evidence which suggests that it could also be due to genetics.

According to geneticists, there may actually be a gene for shyness. Researchers at the University of Colorado and at the Pennsylvania State University observed the behavioral differences between fraternal and identical twins, and came up with some interesting results.

In case you're not aware of the difference, fraternal twins are born at the same time but don't look alike. This is because they share (on average) half their genes. Identical twins, on the other hand, do share the same genetic information, and therefore look alike.

If there is a genetic basis for personality, then identical twins raised in the same home with the same upbringing, should have similar personalities. The anecdotal evidence, however, proves that this isn't the case.

The researchers wanted to understand why one identical twin can be very sociable and adventurous, while the other can be shy and timid. Looking into their genes, they suggest that serotonin could be the cause. Serotonin affects the nervous system, influencing our moods, memory, and learning. Irregular serotonin levels can lead to depression, anxiety, and anti-social behavior, among others.

Geneticist Dean Hamer of the National Institutes of Health, supports this hypothesis. He led a study which suggests a link between the serotonin transporter gene and neuroticism — a personality complex that includes low self-esteem, depression, and extreme shyness. Hamer suggests that a portion of the DNA strand which controls the serotonin transporter could be responsible for neuroticism, an area he calls the "anxiety gene."

Other geneticists believe that extreme shyness and anxiety could be due to a specific gene code: DRD4. This is responsible for a protein that binds dopamine — a chemical messenger that affects the brain.

While these studies suggest a link between biology and personality, doctors also take pains to assert that the environment also plays an important role. In the former case, drugs (such as Prozac™) are often the key to treatment.

Based on these studies, then the fear of rejection might not entirely stem from personal experiences. It could be the result of genetics or other biological factors that modern medical science has yet to understand. If you suspect that this could be the case with you, then consulting a professional might be your best course.

Chapter 2: Understanding the Psychology of Rejection

There are many motivational speakers who say that the fear of rejection is all in the mind, and that strong people should therefore be able to bounce right back. Though comforting in retrospect, the desire to punch such motivational speakers in the face is both understandable and perfectly forgivable. The science proves it, too.

1. Our brains can't distinguish between physical and emotional pain

According to the research, the pain of rejection is very real. Brain scans have shown that specific parts of our brains light up when we get physically hurt. When we feel the pain of rejection, however, those exact same parts of our brains also light up. In other words, our brains can't seem to tell the difference between physical and emotional injury.

Evolutionary scientists believe this could be due to our prehistoric past. To survive in such a brutal age, we needed to belong to a group. Failure to make it into that group (or being kicked out of one) meant that we had to face wild beasts alone, greatly reducing our chances of survival.

While most wild beasts are now behind cages or on the verge of extinction, our brains still interpret rejection as a threat to our survival. Makes sense, in a way. Failure to get that job, promotion, or sale can impact our ability to get food, shelter, and live comfortably, after all. Failure to get that mate, on the other hand, means that our genetic continuity is threatened.

2. Even small forms of rejection hurt a lot

In a rather cruel study, psychologists had a test subject wait with three others in a reception room, ostensibly for a doctor's appointment. The three others were in on the study. One picked up a ball and tossed it to another, who passed it to the third person, who tossed it to the experimental subject.

Without fail, s/he tossed it back to the first person, and it went on for two rounds. On round three, the third person tossed the ball to the first person, completely ignoring the test subject. In each and every case, the victims reported feeling extremely upset, even though they understood how petty it was.

3. Rejection cannot be tempered by reason

The subjects of the above experiment claimed that their emotional pain continued long after the test. Even when they were told that the ball-throwers were experimenters and that there was nothing personal about what they did, many reported feeling depressed for days.

If something so petty such as being kept out of a simple ball-tossing game can hurt for a long time, imagine how much more painful it can be when the stakes are a lot higher.

4. Rejection can temporarily reduce your IQ

In another study, people were asked to take a simple cognitive test to measure their basic IQ. They were then asked to relive a painful experience of rejection and made to take another test. While both tests were similar (only worded and ordered differently), the subjects scored lower on the second test than they did on the first.

5. Our brains respond more strongly to emotional pain

It's been found that people recall emotional pain more vividly than they do physical pain. When those who suffered from debilitating injuries were hooked up to fMRI's and asked to relive the pain they endured, most just shrugged philosophically. When those same people were asked to relive a painful emotional incident, on the other hand, the pain centers of their brains lit up.

This explains why rape victims who recover from their injuries remain traumatized, sometimes for life. Our brains eventually gloss over physical pain. Emotional pain, on the other hand, takes a lot longer to overcome, if at all.

6. Rejection can lead to criminality

According to a 2001 report by the US Surgeon General, the pain of rejection caused more incidents of adolescent violence than drugs, gang membership, and poverty combined. Other studies have shown that it's not limited to adolescents.

People of all ages and genders who've been rejected have taken their aggression out on others, even innocents. And it's not just jilted lovers. Fired employees have also been linked to violent crimes.

7. Rejection can lead to low self-esteem and self-destructive behaviour

Even when attractive people get dumped or rejected by less attractive ones, their sense of confidence can be wrecked. It is believed that this again stems from our prehistoric past, part of our need to belong and to be a part of something.

While these findings can be depressing, it does show that we really are hardwired to take rejection badly. So, the next time you hear a motivational speaker telling you that "it's all in your head," acknowledge it, but understand that we're not designed to snap out of it so easily. Fortunately, there are proven ways to help dull the pain and eventually help us bounce back up.

Chapter 3: How to Handle Getting Dumped

Having someone break up with you is one of the most devastating forms of rejection, especially if you're really into them and if the break up comes out of the blue. Actually, no break up ever really comes out of the blue, so if you're really taken by surprise, then you clearly were not paying attention to the signs (and there are always signs, but we won't cover that here).

That aside, you'll feel awful — shock will turn to disbelief, and when the reality of it finally sinks in, symptoms will include shakiness, guilt, rage, wanting to keel over and die, as well as getting literally sick. In some cases, jilted lovers can actually vomit and develop flu-like symptoms.

Depending on how much emotional investment you've put into the relationship (real or imagined), your physical symptoms can take as long as a week to pass. If it takes a lot longer than that, then you need to seek professional help.

Even if you do, however, the emotional devastation will take a lot longer to go away. Depression, mental dullness, lack of appetite, and lack of vitality can span months, in some cases. During this time, the temptation to visit old haunts, pore over pictures, and listen to music you both enjoyed is likely to send you into crying fits.

While it may seem difficult, most agree that the best solution is to destroy any mementos (especially pictures) that tie you to the past. These things only serve to reinforce the often vain hope you may still be entertaining that there's a chance of getting back together.

Therapists claim that four to six weeks is the average time it takes for most to get over the worst of the depression, after which there should be moments in which things seem better. Again, depending on how much emotional investment you put into the relationship, the good days will still be interspersed with periods of intense depression, but the latter will hit you less and less over the following weeks. In some cases, rage replaces the depression, but those too, should pass.

While there's nothing wrong with isolating yourself in the aftermath of a break up, you can speed up the healing process by not isolating yourself too much. Studies have proven that those who have a network of shoulders to cry on recover faster from the emotional trauma of getting jilted, than those who do it alone.

There will come a moment in which you will achieve what is known as closure. This is when you realize that you no longer feel any emotional connection to the other person. Without realizing it, a day will come when you hear a piece of music you both enjoyed, but it no longer brings about the crying fits.

Please note that six months should really be the maximum grieving time. If you're still feeling awful after that period, there's a good chance that you are suffering from clinical depression. If so, then you really need to get yourself to a therapist.

Before you go that far, however, studies have shown that taking a simple Tylenol can help with the pain of rejection — whether from a job, a promotion, a sale, or a broken heart. In the ball-tossing experiment, they had some subjects take a Tylenol before the procedure, and found that those who did reported less emotional pain than those who didn't.

The experiment to determine the effect of painful memories on IQ levels also made use of Tylenol. They found that those who took a placebo exhibited lower scores than those who took Tylenol.

This is further proof that our brains cannot distinguish between emotional and physical pain. Some feel that those who take anti-depressants are somehow flawed, but the research is showing that this is little different from asthmatics who need to have inhalers.

Chapter 4: Understanding the Fear of Rejection and Failure

Fear of failure is common to all and is very much the same as the fear of rejection. Though it is others who do the rejecting, the one rejected cannot help but feel that they have failed, somehow. While this can be true in some cases, it is not so in all. Whatever the case, the rejected one who takes it the most personally is the one who develops the greatest fear of failure.

Failure causes anger, confusion, disappointment, frustration, guilt, regret, sadness, and shame. And what person doesn't want to protect themselves from such negative emotions? We fear failure because:

1) We're afraid of what people will think about us,

2) We're afraid that they'll lose interest in us,

3) We're afraid of disappointing those whose opinions matter to us,

4) We're afraid that we might not be as smart or as capable as we've been led to believe,

5) We're afraid that we won't achieve our objectives or be able to pursue our dreams, and

6) We're afraid that we'll lose what we already have.

To protect ourselves, therefore, we create defence mechanisms, such as denial. This is the most dangerous coping mechanism of all because though it's easy to spot it in others, it's a lot harder to notice it in ourselves. Denial results in complicated games, such as:

1) Telling ourselves there's no way we could have done things differently,

2) Telling ourselves that it's the fault of others,

3) Telling others not to expect much so as to lower their expectations of us,

4) Procrastinating or showing up too late,

5) Spending more time buying clothes for a job interview instead of studying the company, or spending more time getting study material together rather than actually studying,

6) Spending more time preparing instead of actually doing, and

7) Getting headaches, stomach aches, feeling generally sick, or oversleeping so as to get out of doing something.

You can see from the above that the reasons we fear rejection are the same as our fears regarding failure. Likewise, the mechanisms we use to avoid having to fail are the same ones we use to avoid being rejected. To deal with both, therefore, we have to learn how to handle fear, itself.

Chapter 5: How to Handle Fear and Still Come Out on Top

They say that a brave person is not one who is without fear, but rather, the one who can act despite their fear. A rock thrown into a fire can't possibly feel anything, either physically or emotionally, but fire fighters can, so that saying must have merit.

There are seven ways to get a grip on your fear:

1. Understand that fear is your friend

Fear teaches us to be cautious, which is a good thing for survival, since rock climbing, fire walking, sky diving, and walking alone in darkened alleyways is not a healthy thing. Fear taught you not to talk to strangers, not to put your hand in the fire, or to walk up a flight of steps alone when you were a toddler.

Fear isn't just tied to your physical survival, however. As the studies cited have proven, your brain can't seem to distinguish between physical and emotional pain. Fear is therefore also tied to your ego and to your emotions. It doesn't want you to fail or face rejection because it doesn't want you to get hurt.

You know the difference between physical and emotional pain, even if your brain doesn't. Just as you don't do everything your friends and family say you should, neither should you listen to everything your fear tells you.

2. Consider if the risk is worth it

Proper motivation can make miracle workers of even the most ordinary person. Before you decide to do something you'd rather not, consider if the rewards outweigh the risks.

You might need a job, but before you go around subjecting yourself to an uncomfortable and possibly stressful interview, consider if what you're applying for is something you really want and actually enjoy.

If the job is something you really think you're a fit for, the potential reward should inspire you to move past your discomfort. This will not eliminate the fear nor the possibility of rejection, but it will give you the motivation to act despite the risks involved.

3. Acknowledge your fear and the risks involved

First, you have to own your fear by acknowledging that you can fail and that there will be consequences to your failure. Among these consequences are the feelings of shame and inadequacy, as well as letting others down.

A good way to do this is to write your feelings down. It would be even better if you can talk to others about your concerns, so you can vent and receive some form of emotional support. Again, this will not remove the fear, but it can make you feel less alone, which can provide a tremendous boost to help you act despite your feelings.

4. Find out as much as you can

We're often afraid because we know little about whatever it is we want to go after. The solution is to find out what you can about a situation. If you're going for a job interview, do some research on the company, talk to employees if possible, and so on. The more you understand something, the less alien it becomes, and the less cause you have for fear.

If you're trying to sell something, find out as much as you can about your product, as well as your market. If you're selling to an individual, talk to them to find out what their likes and dislikes are, then tailor your presentation accordingly. If you're selling to an organization, find out their core values and objectives.

5. Plan, but be flexible

Make a list of what you can do, what your limits are, and what strategies you might use to deal with different situations as they occur. Often, our fear arises due to ignorance. We don't know how we'll see something through or what challenges we might face. As such, we fear just getting started.

Once you get as much information as you can, consider how you'll deal with potential scenarios. Brainstorm ideas that might help you succeed. You could be completely wrong, but at least you have a plan. Think of this plan as a map that helps guide you through unknown territory.

If you can't find a job, for example, despite putting yourself on employment sites and regularly poring over classified ads, consider going to social media sites, instead. If the thought of approaching strangers at parties terrifies you, ask friends or family introduce you to people they know.

6. Approach things in small steps

There's a saying which goes, "inch by inch, it's a cinch; yard by yard, it's very hard." Whether you fear new things, new situations, new people, or even rejection, it's probably because you're trying to look at the big picture. If that scares you, then approach it in tiny increments.

Say you want a job. Rather than stress over the interview and the consequences of being jobless, first research the company, potential benefits, and job description. Focus on getting that done. If you are called to an interview, look up interview tips and prepare yourself accordingly.

Your next step is getting to the interview on time, then applying what you learned when you researched how to survive and succeed at interviews. After that, ask your questions (if any), and so on.

The idea behind this is that by breaking the big picture down into small, achievable steps, you also reduce the fear factor down into smaller, manageable chunks. As you get closer to your goal, your confidence rises.

Approaching things in small steps is also a great way to overcome procrastination. Rather than think about how big the task is and how much work needs to be done, breaking it up into smaller and manageable steps provides the psychological boost needed to begin.

7. Focus on the process, not the outcome

Should you fail, see yourself as failing in a certain step, not in failing at the big picture. Don't think, "Oh no, I didn't get the job, now

I'll starve and die." Think instead in terms of, "Well, I didn't make it past that interview, now onto the next one."

The greater your emotional involvement in something, the greater becomes your fear of failure and rejection. By limiting your emotional stake to each step of a process, you mitigate your emotional involvement, and therefore your fear.

Chapter 6: How to Handle Rejection in a Sales Job

Any good marketing person will tell you that success and profitability is a simple numbers game. To get a single "yes," you have to go through an average of about 20 "no's."

This is how the telemarketing game is played and why we're all so annoyed with it. The successful telemarketer, however, also knows that it's a numbers game, so no matter how many times we scream, threaten, and slam the phone down, they'll just keep on calling and calling.

When dealing with others face to face, the luxury of being able to hide behind the anonymity a phone is not there. Fortunately, there are many advantages in dealing with people directly.

Well-trained and well-experienced sales people have been conditioned to dread the "yes" people. These are the ones who will sit through an entire presentation nodding and saying "yes" to everything the salesperson says. What these people are doing is speeding the sales presentation along, so they can get out of there (or get rid of the salesperson) as quickly as possible.

A successful seller wants a client who says "no." This word is valuable, because it allows you to gauge a client's interest (or lack of) in their product or service. So, let's cover the various meanings of "no."

1) "I don't like or trust you"

No matter how good your product is, if the client doesn't like something about you, you're pretty much dead in the water. It's easy to slam the phone down on telemarketers because we can't see them. It's harder to do that to people when they're right in front of you. Proper grooming and proper attire can address this problem, but so can a proper and confident presentation.

Above all, a proper introduction and warm up is important. This means being friendly, trying to get to know more about the person, and really listening to them before you launch into your sales pitch. Doing so will save time and allow you to tailor your presentation accordingly. Most importantly, it allows the customer to see you as a human being and not just as a walking-talking sales pitch.

2) "I'm not interested"

This means you failed in three things: 1) you didn't do prior research on your client, 2) you didn't do a proper warm up, or 3) you didn't tailor your presentation to their needs.

Trying to sell hair care products to bald people is a waste of time, as is to one who is hostile and has no time for a presentation. If you try to do this, then you deserve to be rejected.

3) "I have to think about it"

See number two.

If you know you did everything right and still failed to make a sale, then stay friends and take pains to part on a good footing. Getting into a funk in front of a client who says "no" and sticks to it, is the best way to ruin your reputation.

By remaining friendly with the client, you stand a good chance of getting the names, numbers, and addresses of their friends and family, as well as an introduction.

Remember: this is a numbers game.

Chapter 7: The Proper Attitude for Dealing with Rejection

Since the pain of rejection occurs in the mind, then it's the mind we have to work on — so motivational speakers do deserve some credit, apparently.

Some people seem to take rejection well, or at least bounce back from it fairly quickly. So, what's their secret? Perspective.

Studies have shown that those who have the right perspective recover more quickly from the pain of rejection than those who don't. This is not just about self-esteem, though that also plays a role.

Perspective is how you see the overall picture. A successful salesperson knows from experience that s/he has to go through many "no's" to get to that one "yes." Fresh college graduates know they have to apply to many different companies before they finally get hired. Gamblers know they have to lose some money before they can make any.

Unfortunately, it also means that you sometimes have to have your heart broken (often several times) before you finally find that Mister (or Miss) Right.

None of these successes will ever happen, though, unless you make that first step. In doing so, however, try to see the bigger picture.

Also, consider your expectations and your own self-image. Some people have too high an opinion of themselves, so they take rejection badly. Still others have low self-esteem, so they see rejection as a validation of their worth.

Both are too focused on themselves and not on the bigger perspective. By keeping one's mind on the proper perspective, one can at least mitigate the fear involved, as well as the pain that follows rejection.

Chapter 8: Conquering the Fear of Rejection for Good

There's a not-quite-new program they're teaching in marketing classes and business schools called the *100 No's Challenge*, though some call it the *100 No's List*, as well as *Rejection Therapy*.

Though designed for sales, it can be applied to other things, as well. The point is to make a game of being rejected so you approach it in the spirit of fun while learning to develop a thicker skin.

In this game, you make a list of 100 names to call. Chances are, you'll only make one sale per 100 calls. Say you make that one sale, which earns you a $100 commission. Rather than seeing yourself as getting paid for that one sale, see yourself as being paid $1 per call, which includes those who said "no" to you. Once you understand that "no's" are also profitable, you lessen their negative emotional impact on you.

If selling isn't your forte, then extend the game to other things, and you'll discover miracles.

Perhaps you've seen Jia Jiang's successful YouTube video about going into Krispy Kreme? In it, he plays the Rejection Therapy game by asking Jackie, the manager on duty, to make him a donut set of the Olympic symbol. Jiang expects to be told "no," but Jackie surprises him and becomes a YouTube phenomenon by not only doing it, she gives him the set for free.

To play this game, make a list of 100 things to do that require you to approach people. In his list, Jiang asked a policeman if he could sit in his patrol car, a stewardess if he could make the flight announcement, a homeowner if he could play soccer in his backyard, and some random neighbor if he could watch the Super Bowl game in his house, among others.

To his surprise, Jiang found that he got more "yeses" than "no's." He also found himself amazed at people's kindness, which gave him the courage to launch a successful business. He talks about his amazing experience at a TED talk in Austin, which is definitely worth seeing.

In doing the 100 No's List, Jiang deliberately invited constant rejection and humiliation. It not only strengthened him, however, it also taught him two important things:

1) If you open yourself up to the world, it can open up to you in wonderful and surprising ways, and

2) While it can be embarrassing, uncomfortable, and painful, it can also be incredibly rewarding and empowering.

Conclusion

Understanding that emotional pain is as powerful as physical pain explains why rejection can hurt so much. As with most forms of pain, however, it is manageable. More importantly, it can be overcome with the right attitude and by making a game of it.

We can never escape rejection; it will always crop up in a variety of ways. But just as we develop certain attitudes over time, so we can reengineer the way our minds respond to rejection — or at least, to the fear of it.

It does take time and practice. And if that's not enough, there's always Tylenol.

Finally, I'd like to thank you for reading this book! If you enjoyed it or found it helpful, I'd greatly appreciate it if you'd take a moment to leave a review on Amazon. Thank you!

Printed in Great Britain
by Amazon

46024248R00032